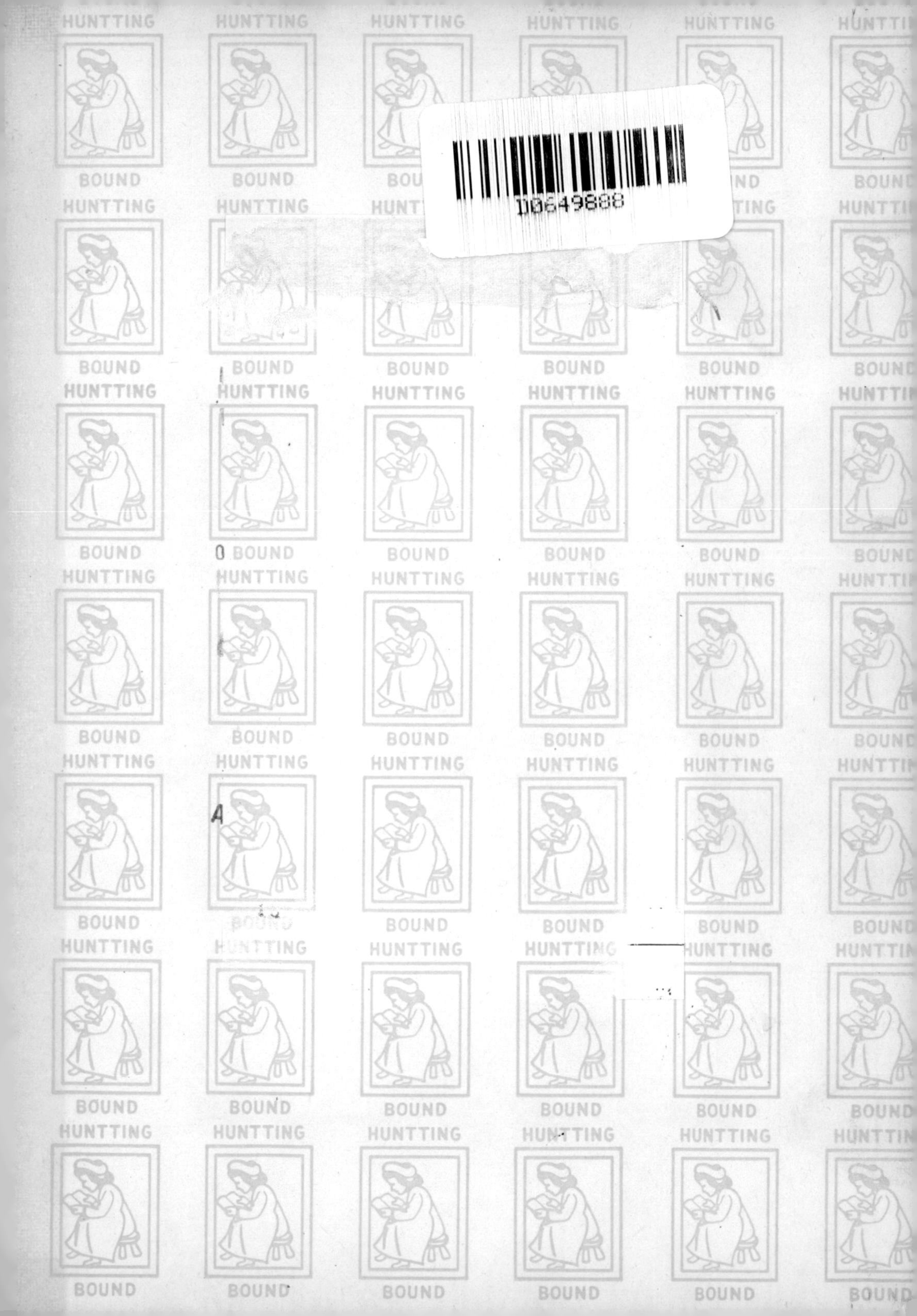

Marco Polo

REAL PEOPLE

Marco Polo

By Ruth Cromer Weir

Illustrated by Rafaello Busoni

Frances Cavanah, *Director of Biographies*

ROW, PETERSON AND COMPANY

EVANSTON, ILLINOIS WHITE PLAINS, NEW YORK

A Boy in Venice

"Good evening, Master Marco Polo!" The owner of the store bowed low. "What brings you to my shop? Can it be that you want cloth for a new jacket?"

A boy had paused before the little shop with its front wide open to the street. He grinned as he bowed low in return. This game was one that he and his friend, the shopkeeper, never tired of playing.

"Why should I want a new jacket?" The boy pulled his own velvet jacket close. "I would much prefer a jewel or some of those rare silks from Asia."

The shop owner glanced proudly at the tables where he kept many treasures for sale. Then suddenly he pretended to be stern. "Young man, how did you know I had just received a new shipment of goods?"

"My nose told me," answered Marco. He sniffed the pleasant odor of spices on the table. There were tiny balls of pepper, roots of ginger plant, and sticks of cinnamon bark. The whole cloves looked like tacks with flower heads.

"You are a smart boy," said the shop owner. "But let us see what kind of a merchant you are going to be. Someday you may carry on trade as your family has always done. Trade is important business. It has made our beautiful Venice the richest city in Italy. Buying and selling brings people from all the world together. Come here, Master Marco."

The shop owner had gone to the back of his store, where he drew a chest from under a table. He unwrapped a small package and placed four stones on the table. "Now, Marco Polo of the noble family of Polo," he said, "can you select and name the most valuable of these jewels?"

The boy looked carefully at a perfect pearl. Beside it was a sparkling sapphire and a piece of smooth green jade. Young Marco picked up the fourth stone. It was a blood-red ruby which seemed to burn with brilliance.

"Sir, I choose this one," he said, without hesitating. "It is a stone fit for a king."

As he looked toward the front of the store, he saw shadows outside. "I must go now. It is getting late. My aunt will worry if I am not home." But he did not leave at once.

"What is it, Marco?" asked the shop owner.

"It's about my father, sir." Marco hesitated. "Do you think he'll ever come back to Venice?"

"Young man, have no fears about your father. I know that he has been gone for a long time, but he and your Uncle Maffeo are wise and clever traders. They'll probably come home one of these days bringing half the riches of Asia with them!" The shopkeeper laughed, for still the boy did not go. "Yes, I know, it is hard to wait. If I ever hear any news—anything at all—I'll come running to your aunt's house to tell you. I promise! Now go before your family starts looking for you."

Venice was a city built on many small islands off the east coast of Italy. The waters of the sea flowed around these islands and formed the canals through the city. By the time Marco left the shop, the sun had set, leaving a pink and blue and purple sky. The colors of the sky were reflected in the water.

"How beautiful," thought Marco. Even the sails on the merchant ships and the marble buildings seemed to turn pink.

On the banks of the canals there were many shops with open fronts like the one Marco had just visited. As he walked toward home, he saw men from many parts of the world. In Venice traders from north, south, east, and west came to carry on business. Long-robed merchants from Palestine or Turkey walked beside men from Scotland wearing short kilts. Traders from other countries in Europe came to Venice to buy silks from far-off China and soft rugs from Turkey. In Venice they could buy rich furs, diamonds, and beautiful shawls. These products were then taken home and sold at a profit.

As Marco passed an open wine shop, he smiled, for he could hear the queer sound of many languages spoken at once. Suddenly he heard a shout in Italian: "Down with Venice and all her fine ways. Down with Venice and her soft-handed nobles. Genoa has the best sailors!"

"Sailors from Genoa must be making trouble again," thought Marco. The people of Genoa on the western coast of Italy were jealous of the power of Venice. The people of Venice were just as jealous of Genoa, which was also an important trading city. When sailors from the two cities came together, there almost always was trouble.

Marco clapped gleefully when two stout sailors of Venice tossed the loud one from Genoa into the street. He landed on the very edge of the canal.

It was growing late, and Marco must hurry home. Soon there would be torches glowing on the canal. The boats called gondolas (*gahn'doh-lahz*) would be moving on the water. The air was warm. Perhaps a big moon would come up later, and there would be soft music.

Suddenly the boy felt lonely. He missed his mother, who had died. Over and over he asked the question, "Will I ever see my father, of whom I have heard so much?" But when he reached his aunt's home, candles were burning brightly as though in welcome. He could smell the spice cakes which he liked to eat. He forgot his loneliness.

Real Adventure Begins at Fifteen

Years passed while Marco waited for his father, Nicolo Polo, and his Uncle Maffeo to come home. He knew that they had been successful traders who had traveled to Constantinople and other cities of eastern Asia. They had left on a trading trip a short time before Marco was born, but they had not returned. No one in Venice had heard from them for many years.

The boy's time was not wasted. He worked in the family's counting house, where he learned about commerce and trade. He learned about different countries and the treasures which came from each. He learned different languages. He learned that in different parts of the world the same product might be worth different prices.

Several times Marco talked to merchants or to sea captains who had been in eastern Asia, but they brought no news of the Polo brothers. "Perhaps they will never come home," he thought. Then one day in 1269, when he was fifteen years old, he heard shouts outside.

"Marco! Marco! They're back," someone called. "Your father has returned. Your uncle has returned."

Marco's merchant friend was leading a group of people. There were merchants, sea captains, and sailors. There were rich people in silks and satins, and poor ones in rags. It seemed that people had popped up from everywhere in Venice. In the center of the crowd Marco saw two tall men. One had dark hair. The other's hair shone red in the sunlight.

As Marco rushed to the street, people stepped aside, leaving a way open. For a moment the dark man stood still in surprise. He could hardly believe that the tall youth was his son. Then he stepped forward and put his arms around Marco's shoulders.

"My son, my son," he said as tears of joy filled his eyes.

Marco had waited years for this day. "Father! Father!" was all he could say. Marco's Uncle Maffeo slapped him on the back, and Marco knew that he was going to like this uncle.

There was great excitement in Venice over the return of the Polo brothers. On their last trading expedition they had decided to try their luck in some of the lands east of Constantinople.

Then a war had broken out. The way back to Constantinople was unsafe for travel, but the way to the East was clear. Marco's father and uncle had traveled farther and farther east until they had finally reached China.

"China!" the people in Venice exclaimed in wonder. Silks and drugs came from China. They were carried on the backs of camels all the way across Asia. European merchants bought them in Constantinople or some other city on the coast. But no one knew very much about the ancient land from which the drugs and shining silks had come. China was six thousand miles away.

"Tell us more!" the people of Venice begged the Polos.

Marco learned that while his father and uncle were in China, they had spent much time at the court of Kublai Khan. Kublai was the khan, or ruler, of a vast empire. The Polo brothers were the first men from Europe that he had ever known. He liked their good manners and their good sense. He wanted to know more about their religion. Therefore he had sent them as his ambassadors to the pope, the head of the Roman Catholic Church. The khan wanted the pope to send a hundred missionaries back to China with the Polo brothers.

Meanwhile, however, the pope had died. The brothers decided to wait in Venice until a new pope was elected. A year went by, then two years, and they could not delay any longer. They made their plans to return to the court of the great khan, and Marco longed to go with them.

Then one day his Uncle Maffeo suggested, "Let's take Marco back with us."

At first Marco's father would not listen to the plan. "It's a dangerous trip," he said. "We must cross mountains and seas and great deserts. Often robbers attack travelers. I will miss the boy, but the trip is too hard."

Marco glanced anxiously at his Uncle Maffeo.

"The boy, as you call him, is better able to stand the trip than you are, my dear brother," Maffeo said. "I find him quite an intelligent young man. He would be a credit to his father in the court of the great khan."

"Good Uncle Maffeo!" said Marco under his breath. When his father finally agreed that he could go, he felt like shouting. "The greatest adventure any boy could have," he thought. "Will the deserts burn as my father and uncle have said? Will there be treasures of shining gold? Will robbers attack us?"

Bandits!

From the beginning Marco found the journey even more exciting than he had dreamed. With his father and uncle he took a ship from Venice for the voyage down the Adriatic Sea and out into the blue waters of the Mediterranean. At last the shores of Palestine came into view. After more weeks of preparations and delays, the three Polos were ready to begin their long, long journey across Asia.

Traveling by land was especially dangerous in those days. Travelers found it safer to go in groups, or caravans, in case they were attacked by bandits. When danger threatened, Marco's father insisted on joining parties of about two hundred or more persons.

Sometimes Marco rode horseback. Sometimes he rode on a camel. He did not seem to mind either the dangers or the hardships of the journey. He was interested in everything that he saw, everything that he heard, and many years later he was to write a book about his adventures. He marveled at some of the unusual customs of the people. As he passed through each new city, he looked at the rich goods offered for sale. He liked to hear about the history and legends of the places the caravans visited.

These lands had once been controlled by the Moslems, followers of the famous religious prophet, Mohammed. Then tribes known as Mongols from the northern plains of Asia had swept down over the land. Other Mongols had conquered China. The great Kublai Khan himself was a Mongol ruler.

Marco's excitement mounted as they came closer to Baghdad. This famous town had been the chief city of the Moslems before the Mongols conquered it. When the Mongol conqueror entered the town, he had found a tower filled with gold, silver, and other treasure. Marco was much impressed by a story that he heard about the Mongol and the Moslem ruler who had loved gold above all other things. Later Marco told this story in his book:

" 'Caliph,' the Mongol conqueror said, 'What did you mean to do with such a huge treasure? Did you not know that I was your enemy and that I was coming with a great host to cast you forth? Why did you not take this gold and silver and use it to pay soldiers to defend yourself and your city?'

"The caliph did not know what to answer. Then the Mongol ordered that the caliph be shut in the treasure tower. 'Now,' he said, 'eat of your treasure as much as you wish, since you are so fond of it. For never shall you have aught else.' "

After four days the caliph died, and Marco ended the story with the words: "Truly his treasure would have been of more service to him had he bestowed it upon men who would have defended his kingdom and his people."

After leaving Baghdad, the Polos traveled through the ancient land of Persia, now known as Iran. In one village where they

stopped, the people worshipped fire. In the old city of Yezd they watched people weaving finest silks. In southern Persia they visited "a fine kingdom named Kerman." Marco later wrote, "Kerman produces turquoises in great abundance, as well as steel and iron. People make harness, swords, and bows. Their arms of every kind are well made indeed."

Marco especially liked to see where and how the treasures of the East were made. He also noticed the crops and animals which the people raised. He saw fruit which he called "apples of paradise," probably much like our oranges. He saw "oxen white as snow," and he traveled over mountains and across plains where it was so cold that one "could scarcely stand it." Before long, as he pressed southward, he found the heat of the sun "tremendous," and the wind "intolerably hot."

The Polos were traveling in the direction of the Persian Gulf. This gulf empties into the Indian Ocean. "Perhaps we can find a ship that will carry us around India," said Marco's father. "Then we can sail on until we reach the kingdom of Kublai Khan. We can avoid the hardships of the desert."

"What's the matter, brother?" asked Maffeo. "Surely *you* wouldn't be complaining about this trip." He flashed Marco a smile. "Marco is the one you said it would be hard for."

It was true that Marco had not complained, although he had found that riding on the back of a camel was the hardest kind of

travel. The swaying and rocking motion of the huge animal often made him feel seasick.

"Some people say camels are called 'ships of the desert' because they carry goods across the desert," Maffeo laughed. "I say they're called ships for quite a different reason. Riding a camel is like riding a rough sea in a storm."

Marco was glad to change to horseback again. Soon he saw the wisdom of traveling with the caravan. Again and again the boy heard the name Nogodar whispered in fear. Nogodar was the king of a great band of robbers who had spread terror for miles around. It was said that as a young man Nogodar had gone to live with an uncle. Then he had run away, taking thousands of his uncle's horses and horsemen. He had conquered a powerful province on the western boundary of India. Nogodar, afraid of nobody, swept across the plains with his followers, robbing and killing wherever he wished.

Marco learned that sometimes the famous bandit had as many as ten thousand horsemen. Riding abreast and keeping close together, they caught every living thing—"man, woman, or beast," —in their path. "Nothing can escape them," an old merchant told Marco. "They butcher the old men whom they capture. The young men and women they sell for slaves."

The anxious travelers pressed on. Even the horses seemed uneasy as the days passed.

"Ride close to me," whispered Marco's father one morning as the three Polos saddled their horses.

A few hours later someone in the group shouted, "Nogodar!" He pointed excitedly to the northeast where a dark cloud seemed to be rising and covering the sky.

"Nogodar! Nogodar! It's his devilish magic," another shouted. "He can bring darkness over the day."

There were cries of terror from the travelers. Most of them raced their horses toward the southwest, making a great cloud of dust. Marco started off with the others. Then suddenly he remembered his father's warning, "Ride close to me."

Terrible thoughts raced through his mind as he wheeled his horse and galloped back to his father. Nicolo Polo had stopped his horse in the desert. Several others had stopped also, waiting to see what he would do.

"What's the matter?" cried Marco. "The bandits! Our companions are leaving us behind."

Nicolo was too busy watching the rising cloud in the northeast to answer. He turned to watch the other travelers riding toward the southwest.

"Follow me," he said at last. "S-l-o-w-l-y! S-l-o-w-l-y!" His voice was calm and steady. Then his black eyes snapped, and he began barking commands. "Break it up now! Don't ride too close! I'll kill the first man who raises a speck of dust!"

Marco had never seen his father so stern. His heart sank when he saw him turn east and just a little south. He was going in an opposite direction from their companions.

It seemed to Marco that they crawled along for hours as the strange black cloud covered the sky. Several times he had trouble keeping his horse from rearing. He could feel a cold sweat trickling down his face and neck. He could see it drop from his nose on his horse's mane. He seemed to live a whole lifetime during the next few hours. All the time he had the feeling that he and his friends were riding into the path of the bandits.

Suddenly a small valley appeared ahead. "Now, ride for your lives!" Marco's father shouted. The riders urged their horses forward, and they raced on and on. Presently the high mud walls of a town could be seen in the distance. Never had there been a more welcome sight.

As the few travelers rested that night in the town, Marco said, "But Nogodar's magic—the blackness—his devilish enchantment. I don't understand it."

"When there are many riders, there is bound to be a great cloud of dust," Nicolo explained. "The dust cloud rises in the sky and seems to cover the sun. Frightened travelers think only of the darkness. They call it magic without stopping to think what causes it."

"Brother Nicolo just tried a little Polo magic," Maffeo added. "Remember your father's command to 'make no dust'? Our fellow travelers made a dust cloud of their own which was easy for the bandits to follow. Meanwhile, as you noticed, we carefully took to the other direction.

"Few people cross Asia safely!" he added. "This isn't the first time we've had to use our heads to save our necks. It won't be the last time."

Days later the Polos reached the ancient city of Hormuz on the Persian Gulf. The men learned there that only they who followed Nicolo had escaped Nogodar and his lawless band. Marco recorded in his book, "The rest were caught, and some of them sold, some put to death."

The Long Road to China

Marco found Hormuz an exciting city. He later wrote, "Merchants come here from India with ships loaded with spicery and precious stones, pearls, cloths of silk and gold, and elephants' teeth." These products were then carried to other countries.

By "spicery," Marco meant much more than spices such as cinnamon, nutmeg, and cloves. He also meant drugs, such as camphor, and dye that was used in coloring cloth. By "teeth," he meant the precious ivory tusks of elephants. "These wares are sold to the merchants of Hormuz," he said, "and in turn they are carried all over the world to be sold again."

It was thrilling to watch the unloading of the ships from India. Marco listened to the merchants in Hormuz arguing about prices. The goods seemed very cheap compared to the prices they would bring in Venice, and Marco was tempted to buy.

Nicolo and Maffeo Polo had planned to make the trip around India by water. When they saw the ships in which they must travel, they shook their heads.

"The planks are held together only with twine made from the husk of the Indian nut," said Marco's father.

"The hulls are held together only with treenails," Marco's uncle pointed out. By treenails he meant wooden pegs or spikes. The people in Hormuz had no iron with which to make nails.

"The ships are wretched affairs," Marco later said. "They have only one mast, one sail, one rudder, and no deck at all."

Marco grinned as he watched one of the ships being loaded. First the cargo was packed tightly in the bottom. Then the cargo was covered with animal skins, or hides. On top of the hides several surprised looking horses were driven. They were to be taken to India and sold. The horses stepped aboard cautiously. There they teetered on the top of the frail little craft, hardly able to keep their balance.

" 'Tis a perilous business to go on a voyage in one of those ships," said Marco with a laugh.

"Yes, and many of them are lost," answered Nicolo Polo. "The storms in this sea are terrible. We'd be fools to try to sail to China in such a frail ship."

Maffeo nodded. "Yes, it will be better to take the long overland route, even though we must cross mountains and burning deserts. And let us be on our way soon."

All three of the Polos were very tired of Hormuz. They were tired of having nothing but dates, salt fish, and onions to eat.

"Hormuz is a sickly place," Marco wrote. "The heat of the sun is tremendous. In the summer a wind often blows across the sands. This wind is so intolerably hot that it would kill every living thing."

One day while the Polos were in Hormuz, just such a wind blew off the desert. On every side Marco saw people rushing toward the nearest streams or lakes. Like the others, the Polos "plunged into water up to the neck and stayed for several hours until the wind had ceased."

A band of soldiers encamped close by was not so fortunate. When the wind began to blow, the men were unable to reach water in time, and they smothered to death. Neither man nor beast could live in that fierce heat. The next day the burned bodies of the soldiers and their horses were found by some of the people from Hormuz.

Soon the Polos joined another caravan moving north. Then they traveled northeast. "The road was long and wearisome," wrote Marco, but after many months they reached a province in northern Afghanistan (*af-gan'ih-stan*). This province was ruled by a king descended from Alexander the Great, who had once conquered the land.

There Marco learned of a mountain where rubies were found among the rocks. No one was allowed to dig in the mountain, except by order of the king, and all the rubies that were mined

there became his property. Other precious stones and silver were also found in this same land. Best of all there were many beautiful swift horses.

Marco was especially interested in the way the people dressed. The men "depended on the skins of beasts for clothing." The ladies wore trousers made of yards and yards of cloth. "This they do to make themselves look large in the hips," said Marco. "The people in Afghanistan consider large hips to be great beauty in a woman." The style of large trousers which Marco noticed can even now be seen where he visited so long ago.

More months passed as the travelers continued to push north and east in central Asia. They crossed mountains so high that the people who lived there called them "the roof of the world." On, on the caravan went. At last it came to the city of Lop on the edge of a great desert in what is now the province Sinkiang (*shin'-je-ahng'*), China.

"Such persons as propose to cross the desert," Marco said, "take a week's rest in this town to refresh themselves. Then they make ready for the journey, taking with them a month's supply of food and water for man and beast. On quitting this city they enter the desert. Here, where it is least wide, it takes a month to cross. 'Tis all composed of hills and valleys of sand, and not a thing to eat is to be found on it."

Strange tales were told of this desert. Sometimes travelers thought that they heard their names called. Others believed that they heard soldiers marching. Still others said that they heard drums or other musical instruments. Perhaps they heard the sound of the wind shifting millions of grains of sand. Or perhaps the loneliness of the desert made them imagine that they heard the sounds. Sometimes people crossing the desert tried to follow the sounds and were lost.

"For this reason," Marco wrote, "travelers keep close together while making the journey. All the animals have bells at their necks so that they cannot easily go astray. At sleeping time a sign is put up to show the direction of the march on the next day."

Nearly three and a half years had passed since Marco left Venice. It seemed as if he had been traveling all his life. He noticed that his father and uncle looked gray with weariness, and their clothes were worn and dusty. Still they pressed on. They were nearing the end of their journey.

Suddenly one day Marco thought that he heard the sound of bells in the distance.

"Father, do you hear something? Uncle, do you hear something?" he asked in alarm. "Perhaps I am just hearing the strange noises of the desert."

Marco's father put his hand to his ear. "No, the sounds you hear are real," he said happily. "They are coming closer. They must be the bells of a messenger for the khan. His messengers often wear bells to announce their coming."

Marco's eyes brightened. His father had told him of Kublai Khan's remarkable postal system. The khan had established postal

stations throughout his kingdom. He employed both horsemen and foot runners to carry news and messages from station to station. In this way he was able to get news from the most distant parts of his provinces.

Before long the tired travelers saw several horsemen galloping toward them. They were indeed the messengers of the khan. When they drew rein before the Polos, the leader of the horsemen said, "The great Kublai Khan has heard of the coming of the honorable men from Venice. He will be happy to welcome his honorable friends from the West at his summer palace, forty days' journey away."

The horsemen escorted the Polos back to the court of the great khan, and the rest of the trip was made in comfort. In every place through which they passed they were treated as honored guests. They were given whatever they needed—food to eat, a place to sleep, horses to ride. At last they reached the magnificent summer palace of the khan.

Never had Marco seen such a beautiful place. Inside, the walls were covered with thin layers of gold and painted with figures of men and beasts and birds and with many different kinds of trees and flowers. These paintings were so lovely that Marco looked at them "with delight and astonishment." He passed through one beautiful room after another and finally reached the great banquet hall.

There the khan and all his court were assembled. The khan sat at a table raised above all the others. On one side of him sat the empress and ladies of the court. On the other side were the men of the court—the khan's sons, relatives, and barons. Every person in the great hall was dressed in silks and jewels.

The Polos knelt before the khan and "paid their respects." He told them to rise. His dark eyes glowed with pleasure. "How did you fare on the way?" he asked.

"We fared well," answered Marco's father, "and our journey ends happily since we find you well and safe."

This courteous answer pleased the khan. He was also much pleased with one of the gifts which the Polo brothers had carried all the way from Jerusalem. They gave him a small jar with a few drops of oil from the light at the tomb of Jesus.

Then the khan noticed Marco, standing tall and handsome behind his father and uncle.

"And who is that you have brought with you?"

Nicolo Polo bowed low. "Sire," he said, " 'tis my own son to honor you."

For several seconds the great khan seemed to study Marco. His eyes said more than his words:

"Welcome is he, too."

In the Service of the Khan

For seventeen years Marco and his father and uncle stayed in China—seventeen years packed with adventure, excitement, and explorations. Kublai Khan admired Marco so much that he sent the young man on important errands or missions. Marco traveled to all parts of the empire and even to other countries on business for the khan.

At court Marco had heard some of the khan's messengers and officers give reports on their trips. The reports were usually dull. Once the emperor had said, "I would far rather hear about the strange sights and the manners of the different countries you have seen than merely to be told of the business you went upon."

Marco's first long trip for the emperor was to the southwest, a journey of six months. When he returned, he reported on the taxes he had collected for the khan. Then he told about the country and rugged mountains. He talked about strange customs of the wild, uncivilized tribes he had seen. In one place he had heard of the custom of inviting a guest to spend the night. During the night the guest was killed. The people believed that the good qualities of the guest would then be given to the master of the house.

The khan's eyes sparkled with interest over these reports. "If this young man live," he said of Marco, "he will surely come to be a person of great worth and ability."

Marco traveled north, south, east, and west. He visited splendid cities larger than any in Europe. He gazed at high temples with shining roofs. He admired beautiful pottery made by the Chinese. He saw "black stones," or coal, being dug out of the mountains to be used for fuel. He saw men trading with paper money and reading printed books. Such things were unknown in Europe at that time.

Marco kept notes of the unusual things that he saw, and he took back interesting reports to the khan. For the first time the khan learned about many of the people that he ruled. He trusted

Marco with more and more important business. He grew very fond of the young Italian, and Marco became one of the most important persons at the court. He dressed in robes made of silk and trimmed with real gold and jewels.

Marco's father and uncle were also helpful to the khan. On one occasion they learned that an ancient city in the southern part of China was holding out against his rule. They then showed his soldiers how to make machines, something like great slingshots, with which to hurl large stones. Through the use of these machines of war, the city and the districts around were captured for the khan.

Meanwhile the Polos were gathering great wealth. By buying and trading, they were able to earn large sums of money. But after seventeen years Nicolo and Maffeo became restless to go back to Italy.

"We have as much wealth as we can carry back with us," said Nicolo one day. "I am homesick for Venice."

"Yes," sighed Maffeo. "I would like to see the sunset on the canals again. The khan grows old. If he should die, it might be hard for us to get out of the country."

He did not say all that he was thinking. There were many at the great khan's court who were jealous of the Polos. To some people, they would always be "foreigners." Often when a ruler died, the foreigners who happened to be in the country were put to death.

Marco also longed to see Venice. He wondered if the sailors of Venice and Genoa were still at odds. Suddenly he was lonely for the friends he had known as a boy.

When the Polos spoke of leaving, the khan objected. "My empire has prospered since you have been here," he reminded them. "No, I cannot part with you."

Nothing more was said, but the Polos did not forget their desire to see their old home again.

Weeks went by, and it was time for the spring hunting trip. Every March, the khan started on a hunting expedition toward the ocean. He rode in a large chamber, or room, supported by four elephants. The inside of the chamber was lined with gold. The outside was covered with the skins of lions.

"Ride beside me, Marco," the khan said one spring day as his large party moved toward favorite hunting grounds. Marco was pleased. To be asked to ride beside the khan was a great honor. "Besides," he thought, "this may be a good chance to mention our return to Venice."

Riding along beside the khan, Marco smiled. He was always amused at the luxury of the khan's hunting parties. At night ten thousand beautiful tents would be pitched to shelter the khan and his barons and the ladies of the court. The tents were lined with rich sable skins. The tent poles were made of the finest polished woods, and the ropes were made of pure silk.

"Your highness—" Marco began.

The khan looked at him sharply, as though reading his thoughts. "Are you unhappy?" he asked.

"No," answered Marco, "but my father and uncle grow older. They would like to see Venice again."

For several minutes the emperor rode along in silence. He seemed tired as he lay on the couch in his chamber. Then he said, "Name anything in my empire, and I shall give it to you, but never again speak of leaving me!"

Just then one of the barons riding on the other side of the khan called out. "Sire! Look out for pheasants!"

He pointed to several long-tailed birds. Instantly the top on the khan's chamber was rolled back. The khan's eyes sparkled. He raised one of his favorite falcons high. The great hunting bird soared. Then it swooped down on its prey.

Marco watched, too, but he did not share the khan's pleasure. He knew that he could never again mention returning to Venice.

The Travelers Return

Before long, however, something unexpected happened to give the Polos their chance to return home. Three ambassadors from far-off Persia arrived at the court. They were on a mission for their khan, Arghun, Kublai Khan's nephew.

"Great khan," they said, "our khan bade us tell you that his wife has died. It was her desire that one of her own family take her place. Therefore, our khan begs that you select one of her relatives in your country to be his new queen."

The emperor suggested Kukachin, a beautiful girl seventeen years old. When the ambassadors saw her, they were delighted. "If we had searched the whole world over, we could never have found a lovelier queen," they said.

Then they became worried. Wars had broken out among the tribes along the route to Persia. The trip would be even more dangerous than usual. It would be a long, hard journey for a girl to take.

"If we could only return on the sea," one of the ambassadors said, "the trip would be faster and safer."

"But alas!" The second ambassador shook his head. "Not one of us knows anything about ships and sailing them."

"Wait! I have an idea." The third Persian's face lighted up. "The Italians! The Polos! 'Tis said they want to go back to Venice. Marco has just returned from India on business for Kublai Khan. He knows the sea. And all three Polos have remarkably good sense. Let us take them."

When the Persian ambassadors asked the great khan about taking the Polos with them, a dark frown crossed his face. He did not want them to leave, but he was not one to do things halfway. He knew that if Marco managed the trip, Kukachin would probably reach his nephew's palace safely.

"He was very loath to let us depart," Marco later wrote, "but at last he did give his permission."

Early in the year 1292 the Polos, Kukachin, the Persian ambassadors, and six hundred others sailed from the east coast of China. Down through the China Sea they went and out into the Indian Ocean. Marco visited lands and islands which no European had ever before seen. Later he told about these places in his book.

It was a long, hard voyage, and nearly two years went by before Kukachin and the Polos finally reached Persia. Several ships had turned back. Others had run into storms at sea and been lost. There had also been much sickness. Of the six hundred persons who had started, only eight finished the voyage. Many had died, including the two Persian ambassadors.

The Polos found that the khan who had sent for Kukachin had also died. They took her to his son, and it was arranged that she

should marry him. Kukachin cried when Marco and his father and uncle left, for she had grown to love them as fathers.

The Polos decided to continue their journey by land. They were furnished with horses and men to escort them on their way. When at last they came to the eastern shore of the Mediterranean, they boarded another ship. Finally in the year 1295 they arrived in Venice.

Marco felt a tingling excitement as he knocked at the door of his old home. The door was opened by the cousin who lived there. Then a shrill voice cried out.

"Go away! Go away! We don't want beggars!"

The Polos looked at one another in surprise. Their clothes looked ragged and dirty after their long journey. They did look like beggars.

The cousin finally allowed them to come in. Other relatives and some of their old friends came to see them. But the Polos had been gone so long and had changed so much that no one knew them. The people in Venice thought that they were frauds.

"You could not possibly be the Polos," they were told. "It has been twenty-four years since they left here. We heard that they had been killed by bandits while trying to cross Asia."

As soon as they were alone, the three Polo travelers threw their arms around one another and laughed until tears came to their eyes. "It must have been Nogodar who killed us!" they said.

Later they invited all their relatives and friends to a great banquet. During the banquet they left the table and changed to silken robes trimmed with hammered gold and jewels brought from China. They had servants bring in the ragged garments which they had worn before. Suddenly, the three travelers began ripping open the seams of their old clothes.

"Oh!" cried the guests.

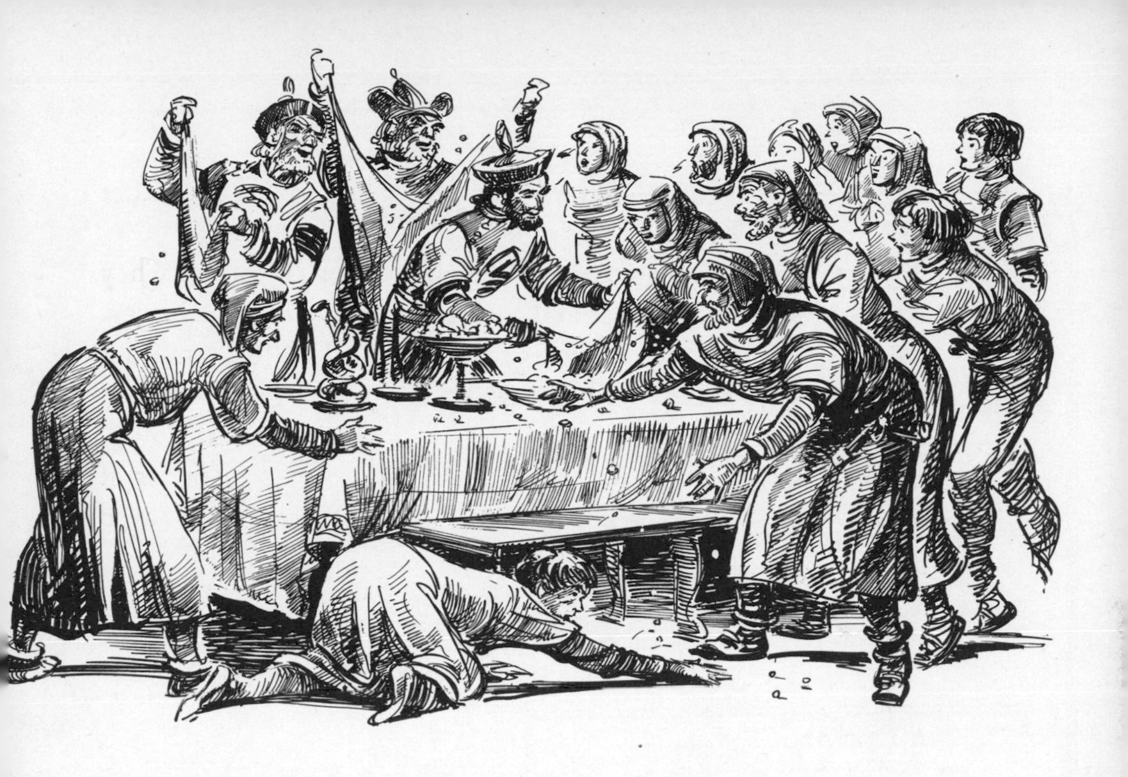

Rubies, emeralds, diamonds, jade, and pearls popped from the seams and rolled over the banquet table and onto the floor. None of the guests had ever before seen so many beautiful and precious jewels. They decided that the three men were not beggars and frauds after all. They were Maffeo, Nicolo, and Marco Polo, who had been given up for dead but by some miracle had returned to Venice.

To Marco, the city seemed little changed. The canals, the shops, and even the complaints about the sailors of Genoa were the same. The old rivalry between the two cities had sharpened into war.

"Alor! Alor!" was the war cry which meant "Fight!" Marco was as loyal to Venice as he had been when a boy, and he took command of a Venetian ship of war known as a galley. In a wild battle in the Mediterranean he was captured with seven thousand others and imprisoned in Genoa.

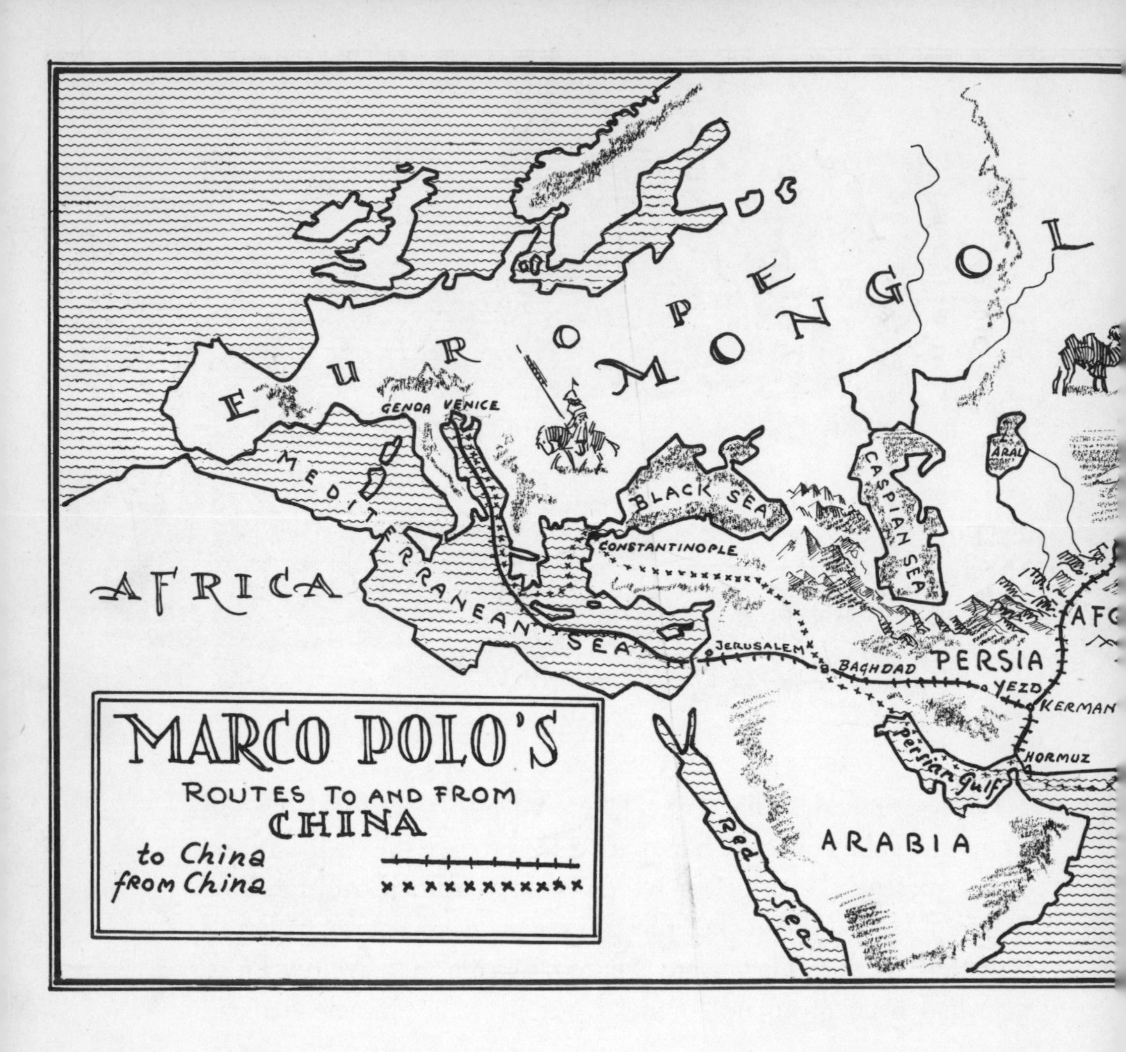

In 1298, while he was in prison, he dictated the story of his adventures to another prisoner who wrote the story down.

The Book of Marco Polo began: "Great Princes, Emperors, and Kings! And People of all degrees who desire to get knowledge of the various races of mankind and of the cities of the world, take this book and cause it to be read to you. For ye shall find therein all kinds of wonderful things."

Marco described his route across Asia. He told about dog sledges used in the north lands bordering the Arctic Ocean. He

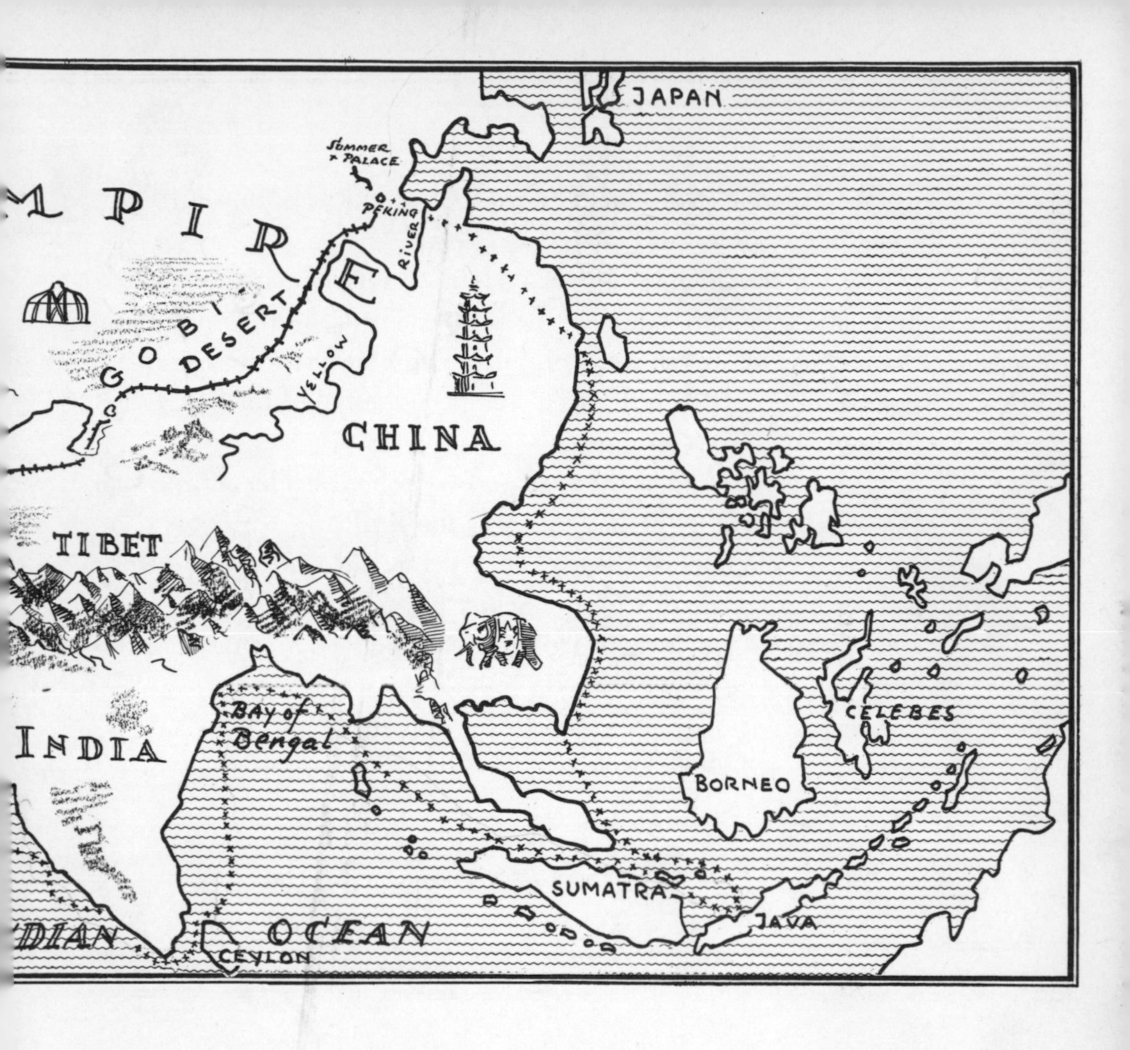

told about naked savages of Sumatra and Nicobar. He told about the wealth of China and Japan. He told where costly diamonds, pearls, rubies, and spices could be found. It was an exciting book filled with the adventures of a real traveler. It told more about a far-off part of the world than had ever before been known.

In 1299 after the Venetian prisoners of war were freed, Marco became famous. Copies of his book could not be made fast enough. Each book had to be lettered by hand since no one in Europe had yet discovered how to print. People throughout the world wanted to read Marco Polo's book, and it was translated into about eighty different languages.

Still, many thought the marvelous things which Marco told must surely be fairy tales. Some people called him the millionaire not because he was so wealthy, but because he used the word millions so often. Before he died, his friends urged him to say that his book was just a fairy story.

He refused. And as the years passed, other travelers found that the wonderful story he had told was the truth.

Marco Polo opened the eyes of a sleepy old world to the treasures that were in the East. Searching for those treasures and easier ways to reach them led later explorers to find new worlds and even greater treasures.

The quotations set off by boldface quotation marks (**"**) are the words used by historical characters in recorded conversations, letters, or documents. Sometimes a quotation has been shortened or adapted to the vocabulary of young readers, but the meaning and style of the original have been carefully preserved.

In a few places the author has told what the character might have said under known circumstances in order to make the biography more vivid. Such imagined conversation is indicated by regular quotation marks (").

TURE CALENDAR OF MARCO POLO AND HIS TIMES

254 MARCO POLO WAS BORN IN VENICE, ITALY

The Mongols had been warring against sections of eastern Europe for nearly twenty years.

The Great Interregnum (1254–1273), a period in Germany when there was no authorized ruler, began.

Louis IX, known for his justice and kindness, was king of France (1226–1270).

271 MARCO POLO STARTED ON HIS JOURNEY TO CHINA

Roger Bacon was telling the people of England and Europe that someday there would be horseless carriages and flying machines.

The last crusade from Europe started for the Holy Land one year earlier.

275 MARCO POLO MET KUBLAI KHAN

Edward I was king of England. From the year 1276 he fought Wales and in 1284 made it subject to the English Crown. The title "Prince of Wales" was given to the heir to the English throne.

292 MARCO POLO LEFT CHINA

Ten years earlier a Danish king was forced to sign a charter, somewhat like the Magna Carta in England.

One year earlier the Crusaders were routed from the Holy Land (1291), but many Christians remained there to carry on trade.

Dante, one of the world's great poets, was living in Italy.

95 MARCO POLO RETURNED TO VENICE

Edward I of England called together nobles, some of the common people, and churchmen to form a group that has since been known as the Model Parliament.

Philip IV, the Fair, was king of France (1285–1314). During his reign a French parliament, called the Estates-General, was established. It included nobles, merchants, and churchmen.

24 MARCO POLO DIED

Edward II was king of England. During his reign Scotland defeated England in the battle of Bannockburn, bringing independence to Scotland that lasted for almost three hundred years.

REAL PEOPLE

BOUND
HUNTTING